WORKBOOK

FOR

STRENGTH IN THE STRUGGLE

A Bible Study Workbook for Women on Letting Go of Fear and Anxiety: A Practical Guide For Implementing Lauren Ibach's Book

WILLOW READS

Disclaimer!!!

This book is a companion book designed for informational and educational purposes only. The content is based on the ideas presented in the main book but it is not endorsed or affiliated with the author or publisher of the main book.

The workbook is intended to complement and enhance the main book, offering readers additional tools for personal growth and self-reflection. However, the workbook should not be considered a substitute for professional advice, diagnosis, or treatment.

While every effort has been made to ensure the accuracy and completeness of the information in this workbook, the publisher and author assume no responsibility for errors, inaccuracies, or omissions.

This book belongs to

_____

_____

_____

Table Of Contents

Introduction

Welcome to the "Workbook For Strength in the Struggle"

This workbook is born out of a deep desire to provide a transformative journey for women seeking solace and strength in the face of life's persistent battles against fear and anxiety. Crafted by Lauren Ibach, an author with a heart for intertwining the profound truths of Scripture with artistic expression, this workbook is a guide to cultivating resilience, trust, and hope in the face of life's challenges.

Why This Workbook Was Created

The world offers myriad solutions to manage fear and anxiety, but "Strength in the Struggle" believes in something far greater—God's Word. This workbook was meticulously designed to help you build a solid biblical foundation for understanding fear and anxiety. Lauren Ibach invites you to explore the transformative power of Scripture, offering not just theoretical knowledge but practical tools to face your struggles head-on. Through ten comprehensive lessons, each centered around a memory verse, you'll embark on a journey that combines the richness of God's Word with the beauty of hand-lettered illustrations, short commentaries, and thoughtful questions.

Benefits of the Workbook

Biblical Understanding: Gain a deep, nuanced understanding of fear and anxiety through a biblical lens, allowing the truths of Scripture to reshape your perspectives.

Practical Application: Move beyond theoretical knowledge to practical application. Each lesson equips you with tools to apply God's Word in real-life situations, fostering resilience and strength.

Artistic Engagement: Immerse yourself in the beauty of artistic reflections, with hand-lettered illustrations that enhance your memorization and meditation experience.

Community and Dialogue: Whether you're engaging in individual study or participating in a group, the workbook fosters a sense of community. Share insights, discuss thoughtful questions, and grow together in faith.

How to Use the Workbook

Start with Prayer: Begin each session with prayer, inviting the Holy Spirit into your study. Acknowledge your struggles and surrender them to God, seeking His guidance and illumination.

Engage Thoughtfully: As you progress through each lesson, engage thoughtfully with the Scripture, illustrations, and commentaries. Reflect on the provided questions, promoting critical thinking and personal introspection.

Memorize and Meditate: Embrace the practice of memorizing and meditating on Scripture. Internalize the memory verses, allowing them to become a source of strength in moments of fear and anxiety.

Create Artistic Expressions: Embrace the artistic reflections provided in the workbook or create your own. Use this creative process as a form of meditation and expression, deepening your connection with key passages.

Share in Community: If you're part of a group study, share your insights, artistic expressions, and reflections. Embrace the diversity of perspectives within the group, fostering rich and meaningful discussions.

Apply in Daily Life: Take the principles learned in each lesson and apply them to your daily life. Consider how God's Word can guide your decisions, shape your responses, and bring about transformative change.

Cultivate Continual Prayer: Beyond the workbook, cultivate a continual prayerful attitude. Let your ongoing dialogue with God permeate every aspect of your life, anchoring you in His peace and strength.

"Strength in the Struggle" is not just a workbook; it's a guide to discovering profound strength in the midst of life's struggles. May this journey lead you to a deeper trust in Jesus and His promises, providing lasting hope and resilience.

Overview Of The Main Book

"Strength in the Struggle" by Lauren Ibach is a transforming Bible study workbook for ladies wanting to overcome fear and anxiety through a deeper relationship with Christ. With ten thorough lessons, this 92-page workbook presents a broad investigation of biblical ideas, encouraging readers to discover courage in the face of life's struggles.

The trip starts with a biblical examination of fear and worry. The author helps readers comprehend these emotions from the perspective of Scripture, laying a firm basis for the transforming journey ahead. The workbook emphasizes that, although the world provides numerous answers, the genuine source of strength is Jesus and His Word.

The acknowledgment of the power of God's Word in bringing about change is a significant subject throughout the workbook. Each of the ten classes is centered on a unique memory verse that has been carefully picked for its relevance to the difficulties of fear and anxiety. The verses are not only written inside the workbook for a convenient reference but they are also ornamented with hand-lettered artwork, boosting the memory process and adding an artistic component to the study.

The workbook guides readers to anchor their trust in Christ's promises as a key focus. This section looks at how the gospel may be used to overcome fear and anxiety. The workbook is interlaced with lessons focused on implementing God's Word in everyday life. Readers are given practical ways to incorporate biblical concepts into their ideas and behaviors, resulting in long-term transformation.

Another chapter emphasizes the need to memorize significant passages and meditate on Scripture. The workbook gives practical strategies to help memory, and understanding the importance of internalizing God's Word on spiritual development.

The creative aspect of the workbook is reinforced with hand-lettered drawings of crucial chapters. These creative reflections not only help with memorizing but also provide a distinctive and intriguing element to the study. Contextualizing memory passages within their historical and biblical contexts deepens the reader's knowledge, promoting a stronger connection to the verses and their importance.

Each lesson is accompanied by a short commentary that provides clarity and insight into the passages being examined. These comments help to improve understanding and give practical applications for real-life situations. Thought-provoking questions are intentionally included to help readers dive further into each text, stimulating personal reflection and enabling group conversations.

The latter chapters concentrate on the spiritual aspect of the subject. Prayer prompts are offered to assist readers in asking the Holy Spirit to work through each lesson, acknowledging the need for supernatural assistance and change in the fight against fear and anxiety. In essence, "Strength in the Struggle" is a comprehensive and uplifting resource that blends biblical insight, creative expression, and practical application to guide women to greater confidence in Jesus and the hope that He provides. This workbook is more than simply an academic study; it is an invitation to a transforming journey of faith that will provide strength for the inevitable hardships of life.

Biblical Perspectives on Fear and Anxiety

Key Takeaways

Establish a firm biblical basis for understanding fear and anxiety. Examine major Scriptures that address these emotions, diving into their historical and cultural settings to obtain a better understanding of their significance.

Worldly vs. Biblical Perspectives: Compare and contrast the world's remedies to fear and anxiety with the biblical viewpoint. Highlight the limits of earthly ways and the transcendent power and authority of God's Word in changing lives.

Identification and Definition: Encourage self-reflection by assisting readers in identifying particular instances of dread and anxiety in their lives. Define these emotions in the context of Scripture, promoting a clear knowledge of the issues at hand.

Personal link: Make a personal link with the biblical content by allowing readers to relate their own experiences with fear and anxiety. Create a feeling of camaraderie inside the workbook by recognizing that many people suffer from similar emotions.

scripture Promises: Introduce the notion of depending on scripture promises to battle fear and anxiety. Examine chapters that directly give consolation and confidence, setting the framework for accepting God's Word as the ultimate source of strength.

Lay the framework for practical application by addressing how biblical learning may be translated into everyday life. Give instances of how certain Scriptures might be utilized in different circumstances, developing a proactive attitude to conquering fear and anxiety.

Personal Commitment: End the chapter by asking readers to make a personal commitment to handling fear and anxiety from a biblical viewpoint. Encourage them to consider how this commitment corresponds with their goal for long-term change.

Reflection Questions

How would you define your present knowledge of dread and anxiety, and how has it been shaped by the world around you?

_____

_____

_____

_____

_____

_____

_____

_____

Can you recall particular moments in your life
when fear or anxiety posed a substantial
challenge? What were the conditions, and how did
you react?

_____

_____

_____

_____

_____

_____

_____

In what ways do you recognize the limits of worldly remedies to fear and anxiety? How can a biblical worldview provide anything more?

_____

_____

_____

_____

_____

_____

_____

Share an experience with dread or anxiety in which you sensed a personal connection to a biblical scripture. What was the text, and how did it affect your perspective?

_____

_____

_____

_____

_____

_____

_____

_____

Consider particular scripture promises that speak
to you in the context of fear and anxiety. How may
these promises provide you peace and assurance?

_____

_____

_____

_____

_____

_____

_____

_____

Consider a realistic circumstance in which you may use a biblical concept presented in this chapter. What measures can you take to incorporate God's Word into your everyday life?

_____

_____

_____

_____

_____

_____

_____

God's Word's Transformational Power

Key Takeaways

Explore the notion of Scripture as alive and active, capable of bringing about revolutionary change in people. Emphasize the dynamic aspect of God's Word and its significance to personal progress.

Introduce memorization as a spiritual practice and as a valuable technique for internalizing Scripture. Discuss the advantages of memorizing important passages and the effect it might have on one's thinking.

Transformational Testimonies: Share the stories of those who have been transformed by the power of God's Word. Highlight particular occasions when remembering and concentrating on Scripture helped you overcome obstacles.

Application of Memorized passages: Assist readers in applying the passages they have memorized to real-life circumstances. Show how these memorized texts may be a source of strength and wisdom in times of fear and worry.

Examine the relationship between Scripture and identity, highlighting how internalizing God's Word influences one's self-perception. Discuss texts that support one's identity in Christ and oppose fear-based narratives.

Cultivating a Memory Practice: Provide practical advice and tactics for developing a regular memory practice. Provide suggestions for making Scripture memorizing a pleasurable and sustainable part of everyday life.

Celebrating Transformation: Finish the chapter by recognizing examples of transformation via God's Word. Encourage readers to share their stories and reflect on the good improvements they've seen in their lives.

Reflection Questions

How do you now see the transformational influence of God's Word in your life? Where do you see the opportunity for development via Scripture?

_____

_____

_____

_____

_____

_____

Consider memorizing as a spiritual exercise. How could memorizing verses help you connect with God and His Word?

_____

_____

_____

_____

_____

_____

Have you heard testimonials of people who were transformed by Scripture? How have these tales changed your view on the power of God's Word?

_____

_____

_____

_____

_____

_____

_____

_____

Consider a particular scripture you've learned and applied to a real-life scenario. What was the verse, and how did it affect your reaction to dread or anxiety?

_____

_____

_____

_____

_____

_____

_____

_____

Examine scriptures that speak to your identity in Christ. How might these verses help you modify your self-perception and resist fear-based narratives?

_____

_____

_____

_____

_____

_____

If memorizing is a new exercise for you, what practical actions can you take to establish a consistent memorization routine? How can you make this practice more pleasurable and sustainable?

Trusting the Gospel as the Ultimate Hope

Key Takeaways

Establish a firm grasp of the core message of the gospel. Examine significant scriptures that describe the essential beliefs of the Christian faith, stressing the hope given in Christ.

Examine how the gospel truths directly combat the roots of fear and worry. Discuss particular components of the gospel that bring hope and confidence in difficult situations.

The Unchanging Nature of God: Consider God's unchanging nature as a source of peace and assurance. Examine biblical texts that illustrate

God's faithfulness and how this reality aids in conquering fear.

Yielding Control to God: Discuss the notion of yielding control to God and how it relates to finding peace in the face of terror. Examine biblical instances of people who gave their worries and concerns to God.

The Role of Faith: Investigate the role of faith in believing the gospel as the ultimate hope. Discuss texts that emphasize the link between faith and conquering fear, highlighting the reliability of God's promises.

Practical methods for Trusting the Gospel: Provide readers with practical methods to actively trust in the gospel in their everyday lives. Discuss attitudes and actions that promote a mentality of hope and dependence on Christ.

A personal perspective on Gospel Hope: End the chapter with a personal perspective on the hope contained in the gospel. Encourage readers to chronicle their ideas and experiences, strengthening the link between the gospel and conquering fear.

Reflection Questions

How would you express the essential message of the gospel in your own words? In what ways does this message deliver hope and certainty in times of fear?

_____

_____

_____

_____

_____

_____

_____

Consider particular portions of the gospel that directly combat the roots of fear. How have these principles changed your view on difficult circumstances?

_____

_____

_____

_____

_____

_____

Consider verses that demonstrate God's unchanging character. How can appreciating God's faithfulness help you overcome fear and anxiety?

_____

_____

_____

_____

_____

_____

_____

Investigate the idea of giving control to God. Is there anything in your life where giving control might provide you calm in the face of fear?

_____

_____

_____

_____

_____

_____

_____

_____

Consider the role of faith in believing the gospel as the ultimate hope. What verses about confidence and trust in God's promises speak to you personally?

_____

_____

_____

_____

_____

_____

_____

_____

What practical measures can you take to actively trust in the gospel in your everyday life? How might habits and actions build an attitude of hope and dependence on Christ?

_____

_____

_____

_____

_____

_____

_____

Journal your own thoughts on the gospel's message of hope. How has your understanding of gospel hope changed, and how has it informed your attitude to dread and anxiety?

_____

_____

_____

_____

_____

_____

_____

Using God's Word in Daily Life

Key Takeaways

Clarify the notion of implementing God's Word in everyday life. Discuss the application of biblical concepts in daily settings and their possible effect on decision-making.

discovering related Scriptures: Assist readers in discovering Scriptures that are immediately related to their everyday concerns. Examine texts that provide insight and wisdom in handling many facets of life.

Journaling for Reflection: Introduce journaling as a tool for reflection and application. Discuss the advantages of capturing ideas and insights received from Scripture study and how it leads to personal development.

Integrating Bible Study into Routines: Provide ways for incorporating Bible study into everyday routines. Discuss how constancy in studying God's Word adds to transforming and meaningful everyday life.

Discuss the significance of sharing biblical ideas with others. Investigate the notion of community and how communal reflection may improve knowledge and inspire responsibility.

Provide practical examples of how certain biblical ideas might be implemented in real-life circumstances. Using real instances, demonstrate the transformational impact of God's Word.

Continuing Commitment to Application: End the chapter by highlighting the significance of a continuing commitment to implementing God's Word. Encourage readers to make conscious decisions that are consistent with their increasing biblical knowledge.

Reflection Questions

How do you now handle the notion of implementing God's Word in your everyday life? Where do you see larger application potential?

_____

_____

_____

_____

_____

_____

Consider certain Scriptures that may directly address issues you confront in your everyday life. How may these texts help you make decisions?

_____

_____

_____

_____

_____

_____

_____

Consider the advantages of journaling for reflection and application. How may writing down your ideas and observations help you develop as a person?

_____

_____

_____

_____

_____

_____

_____

_____

Investigate methods for incorporating Bible study into your everyday routine. How does constancy in studying God's Word affect the transforming quality of your everyday life?

_____

_____

_____

_____

_____

_____

_____

_____

Share your ideas on the significance of sharing biblical insights with others. How might collective reflection within a community increase your knowledge and encourage accountability?

_____

_____

_____

_____

_____

_____

Consider practical instances of how you may apply certain biblical ideas in real-life circumstances. In specific instances, how have you seen God's Word's transformational power?

_____

_____

_____

_____

_____

_____

_____

Scripture Memorization and Meditation

Key Takeaways

The Importance of Memorization: Examine the relevance of memorizing Scripture as a method of internalizing God's Word. Discuss how memory helps spiritual development and prepares people to handle problems.

Examine biblical instances of people who memorized and reflected on Scripture. Discuss how this practice affected their faith and perseverance in the face of hardship.

Memorization strategies: Provide realistic memorization strategies to assist readers in memorizing important verses. Discuss several techniques to accommodate diverse learning styles and preferences.

Benefits of Meditation: Emphasize the advantages of meditation in combination with memorizing. Investigate how meditation builds a feeling of connection with God and increases awareness.

Adopting Memorization into Daily Life: Assist readers in adopting memorization into their daily lives. Discuss how to smoothly include Scripture memorization into routines and activities.

Scripture Memory Obstacles: Recognize possible obstacles in Scripture memorizing and suggest ways for overcoming them. Encourage perseverance and patience in developing this vital spiritual practice.

Reflection on remembered passages: End the chapter by urging readers to think about the passages they've remembered. Investigate how these verses have influenced their cognitive processes and reactions to fear and anxiety.

Reflection Questions

How do you now see the importance of Scripture memorization in your spiritual journey? How may memorizing help you develop spiritually?

_____

_____

_____

_____

_____

_____

_____

Consider biblical instances of people who memorized and concentrated on the Bible. How did this practice affect their faith and perseverance in the face of adversity?

_____

_____

_____

_____

_____

_____

_____

Examine many remembering strategies to find one that works for you. How can you implement this strategy into your routine for successful Scripture memorization?

_____

_____

_____

_____

_____

_____

_____

_____

Consider the advantages of meditation in combination with memorizing. How may a daily meditation practice increase your comprehension of Scripture and develop a feeling of relationship with God?

_____

_____

_____

_____

_____

_____

_____

_____

Share practical ways you might apply Scripture memorizing to your everyday life. How do you incorporate memorizing into your daily routines and activities?

_____

_____

_____

_____

_____

_____

Recognize probable difficulties with Scripture memory. What techniques can you use to overcome these obstacles, and how might tenacity help you succeed in this field?

_____

_____

_____

_____

_____

_____

_____

Artistic Reflections: Hand-Lettered Illustrations

Key Takeaways

Examine the function of art in memorizing. Discuss how hand-lettered drawings improve memory and offer a visually appealing experience.

Provide insight into the artistic interpretation of significant passages. Discuss the process of picking passages for illustration and how visual components may increase the understanding of Scripture.

Visual and Kinesthetic Learning: Recognize the variety of learning styles by stressing the advantages of visual and kinesthetic learning.

Discuss how the mix of art and Scripture supports different learning styles.

Creating Personal Creative Expressions: Encourage readers to create their own creative interpretations of Scripture. Discuss the therapeutic and contemplative components of creative involvement, as well as how it might improve one's relationship with God's Word.

Discuss the importance of art in group study environments. Investigate how creative expressions might promote cooperation, conversation, and a shared experience of Scripture.

Art as a Tool for Reflection: Emphasize the importance of art as a tool for reflection. Encourage readers to interact with hand-lettered pictures as a way of focusing on and internalizing the verses they represent.

Appreciation for creative variety: End the chapter by encouraging an appreciation for creative variety. Encourage readers to appreciate varied creative interpretations and discover personal significance in the visual expression of Scripture.

Reflection Questions

How do you now see the importance of art in assisting memorization? How might hand-lettered images enrich your reading of Scripture?

_____

_____

_____

_____

_____

Consider the artistic interpretation of significant texts. How could visual elements increase the understanding of Scripture for you?

_____

_____

_____

_____

_____

_____

Consider your learning style. How does the mix of art and Scripture meet your tastes, especially in terms of visual and kinesthetic learning?

_____

_____

_____

_____

_____

_____

Encourage yourself to produce your own creative interpretations of Scripture. How can creative expression help you comprehend and connect with God's Word?

_____

_____

_____

_____

_____

How might creative expressions enhance group cooperation, conversation, and a shared experience of Scripture?

_____

_____

_____

_____

_____

_____

How may hand-lettered pictures be used to meditate on and internalize the passages they represent?

_____

_____

_____

_____

_____

_____

_____

How does this appreciation help you understand and connect with the many ways individuals interact with Scripture?

_____

_____

_____

_____

_____

_____

Contextualizing Memory Verses

Key Takeaways

Importance of Context: Stress the significance of knowing the context of memory verses. Discuss how historical and biblical context improves interpretation and enriches the meaning of Scripture.

Verses' Cultural Relevance: Look at the cultural significance of memory verses. Discuss how cultural context impacts Scripture interpretation and adds to a more sophisticated understanding.

Avoiding misunderstanding: Provide advice on how to avoid misunderstanding by taking context into account. Discuss frequent problems in understanding solitary passages and how contextualization avoids misapplication.

Examine the historical relevance of memory poems. Discuss how being aware of historical events and locations enhances the reader's relationship with Scripture.

Application of Context in Study: Assist readers in applying contextual knowledge to their studies. Discuss practical techniques for studying and combining historical and biblical background into verse interpretation.

Collaborative Contextualization: Discuss the advantages of collaborative contextualization in group study. Investigate how different views lead to a more complete knowledge of memory verses.

Personal Connection via Context: Finish the chapter by emphasizing the personal connection readers may have with memory verses through context. Encourage readers to evaluate how historical and biblical context influences their understanding and application of Scripture.

Reflection Questions

Consider how important it is to grasp the context of memory verses. How has considering context enriched your knowledge and interpretation of Scripture?

Consider the cultural significance of memory poems. How does the cultural environment impact your reading of Scripture, and how could this expand your understanding?

_____

_____

_____

_____

_____

_____

Consider the risks of misunderstanding and the significance of context in preventing them. How might a knowledge of context help to avoid the misuse of isolated verses?

_____

_____

_____

_____

_____

_____

_____

Investigate the historical relevance of memory poetry. How can being aware of historical events and places help you connect with Scripture?

_____

_____

_____

_____

_____

_____

Consider practical techniques to include contextual awareness in your research. How can you explore and combine historical and biblical background into verse interpretation?

_____

_____

_____

_____

_____

_____

Consider the advantages of collaborative contextualization in group studies. How can different points of view assist in a more thorough knowledge of memory verses?

_____

_____

_____

_____

_____

_____

_____

How does the historical and biblical context influence your understanding and application of Scripture? How might this personal connection increase your engagement with God's Word?

_____

_____

_____

_____

_____

_____

Clarity Through Brief Commentaries

Key Takeaways

The Role of Commentators: Examine the role of commentators in clarifying Scripture. Discuss how brief commentary may provide insights, historical context, and practical applications, boosting the reader's knowledge.

Personal Interpretation: Emphasize the balance between personal interpretation and external discoveries. Assist readers in determining when to seek further opinions and how to blend other viewpoints with their own contemplation.

Recognizing theological Themes: Discuss how brief commentary might assist readers in recognizing theological themes inside texts. Investigate the value of knowing bigger theological themes in interpreting individual texts.

Application to Real-Life circumstances: Show how brief comments contribute to the application of Scripture in real-life circumstances. Give instances of how external ideas might help you navigate issues.

Short remarks highlight the accessibility of theological learning. Discuss how these tools might help readers connect with religious topics in a more accessible and meaningful manner.

Provide advice on how to choose reputable commentary. Discuss standards for judging the credibility of external materials, emphasizing prudence in selecting commentaries that agree with biblical values.

Encourage discussion in Group Studies: Finish the chapter by fostering discussion in group studies. Discuss how sharing and discussing brief comments in a group context might deepen the collective knowledge of Scripture.

Reflection Questions

Consider the importance of commentaries in your Bible study. How have commentaries aided your comprehension, and how have they changed your interpretation?

_____

_____

_____

_____

_____

Consider the relationship between personal interpretation and external insights. When do you find it useful to seek extra feedback, and how do you incorporate other viewpoints into your own reflection?

Examine the identification of religious concepts via brief remarks. How has your comprehension of bigger theological themes changed your reading of individual verses?

_____

_____

_____

_____

_____

_____

Consider realistic instances of how brief commentary has aided in the application of Scripture in real-life circumstances. In what ways have external ideas offered practical advice in handling challenges?

_____

_____

_____

_____

_____

Consider the accessibility of theological learning via brief remarks. How have these tools helped you connect with religious themes in a palatable and meaningful way?

_____

_____

_____

_____

_____

Consider your criteria for finding reputable remarks. What variables do you examine when determining the trustworthiness of external resources, and how might discernment help you make decisions?

_____

_____

_____

_____

_____

_____

Encourage discussion in your group study. How might sharing and discussing brief remarks in a group context improve the collective comprehension of Scripture? How might different points of view help to a better understanding?

_____

_____

_____

_____

_____

Thoughtful Questions to Deepen Study

Key Takeaways

Establish the aim of insightful inquiries in increasing your study of Scripture. Discuss how well-crafted questions foster contemplation, investigation, and a deeper connection with the material.

Investigate how meaningful questions foster critical thinking. Discuss the significance of questioning, challenging assumptions, and obtaining a deeper grasp of the underlying message.

Connecting Verses to Life Application: Demonstrate how thoughtful inquiries promote the connection between verses and real-life applications. Discuss instances of questions that inspire readers to evaluate how Scripture pertains to their everyday lives.

Encourage Personal Reflection: Discuss the importance of insightful questions in stimulating personal reflection. Investigate how questions might motivate readers to reflect, leading to personal discoveries and spiritual progress.

Developing Group Discussion: Emphasize the importance of intelligent questions in developing group conversations. Discuss how group members might offer varied viewpoints to create a rich atmosphere for collective inquiry and learning.

Balancing Open-Ended and Guided inquiries: Provide advice on how to balance open-ended and guided inquiries. Discuss how combining both sorts of questions improves the study experience by allowing for inquiry while still offering structure.

Creating Unique Questions: End the chapter by asking readers to generate unique questions. Discuss the empowerment that comes from tailoring questions to individual needs and areas of concentration.

Reflection Questions

Consider the significance of insightful questions in your Bible study. How have well-crafted questions aided your reflection and enhanced your engagement with the text?

_____

_____

_____

_____

_____

_____

How have questioning and challenging assumptions helped you get a better grasp of the underlying meaning of Scripture?

_____

_____

_____

_____

_____

Consider these examples of intelligent inquiries that relate verses to real-life applications. How have these questions inspired you to evaluate the practical implications of Scripture in your everyday life?

_____

_____

_____

_____

_____

_____

_____

Consider the importance of meaningful questions
in stimulating personal introspection. How have
questions led you to reflect, resulting in personal
discoveries and spiritual growth?

_____

_____

_____

_____

_____

Consider the usefulness of intelligent questions in group conversations. How has group conversation increased your knowledge of Scripture, and how have different viewpoints contributed to the collective exploration?

Consider the balance between open-ended and directed inquiries. How can this combination improve your study experience by allowing for exploration while yet offering structure?

_____

_____

_____

_____

_____

_____

Consider the power that comes from generating personalized queries. How might creating questions targeted to your specific needs and areas of interest improve your Bible study?

_____

_____

_____

_____

_____

Inviting the Holy Spirit: Prayer and Reflection

Key Takeaways

Recognizing the Holy Spirit's function: Explain the importance of recognizing the Holy Spirit's function in Bible study. Discuss how prayerful reliance on the Holy Spirit improves knowledge and application of Scripture.

Explore prayer as a two-way conversation with God. Discuss the significance of not just delivering requests but also listening for direction and insights during prayer.

Inviting the Holy Spirit into learning: Show how prayer may directly welcome the Holy Spirit into the learning process. Discuss the transformational power of seeking the Holy Spirit's direction and enlightenment.

Aligning learning with God's plan: Discuss how prayer aligns the learning process with God's plan. Examine the idea of surrendering one's studies to the Lord and seeking alignment with His intentions.

Personal and Group Prayer Practices: Provide direction on personal and group prayer practices in the context of Bible study. Discuss how combining prayer with individual and group learning produces a spiritually rich atmosphere.

Reflection as a Form of Prayer: Investigate reflection as a form of prayer in the context of Bible study. Discuss how reflective activities help to a closer relationship with God and a more comprehensive comprehension of Scripture.

Cultivating a Continuous Prayerful Attitude: End the chapter by urging readers to adopt a continuous prayerful attitude. Discuss how a continual conversation with God may pervade all parts of their life, including their study of Scripture.

Reflection Questions

In what ways has prayerful reliance on the Holy Spirit aided your knowledge and application of Scripture?

_____

_____

_____

_____

_____

How do you approach prayer as a conversation, actively listening for advice and insights throughout your time of connection with God?

_____

_____

_____

_____

_____

_____

How has seeking the Holy Spirit's direction and enlightenment changed your understanding of Scripture?

_____

_____

_____

_____

_____

_____

In what ways do you submit your studies to the Lord and seek harmony with His intentions via prayer?

_____

_____

_____

_____

_____

_____

How have these activities contributed to a spiritually rich atmosphere for your research?

_____

_____

_____

_____

_____

_____

How can reflective practice lead to a closer relationship with God and a more comprehensive grasp of Scripture?

_____

_____

_____

_____

_____

_____

_____

How may a continual conversation with God
pervade all parts of your life, including your study
of Scripture? How may this mindset benefit your
spiritual journey?

_____

_____

_____

_____

_____

_____

_____

Final Evaluation Questions

How has your knowledge of fear and anxiety changed throughout the course of this study?

_____

_____

_____

_____

_____

_____

_____

In what ways have you found memorizing and meditation practices to be beneficial in internalizing Scripture and conquering fear?

_____

_____

_____

_____

_____

_____

_____

Consider particular situations when the gospel truths brought hope and certainty in the face of dread. How has your faith in the gospel grown?

_____

_____

_____

_____

_____

_____

_____

How have you used the ideas from this research to combat fear and anxiety in real-life situations?

_____

_____

_____

_____

_____

_____

_____

_____

Examine the effect of incorporating the historical and biblical context on your interpretation of memory passages. How has context influenced your understanding?

_____

_____

_____

_____

_____

_____

_____

How have brief comments improved your understanding of Scripture by providing clarity and insight?

_____

_____

_____

_____

_____

_____

_____

_____

Consider the importance of smart questions in
your research. How have they fostered critical
thinking and textual exploration?

_____

_____

_____

_____

_____

_____

_____

Share your experiences with prayer and meditation in the context of Bible study. How has letting the Holy Spirit into your studies benefited your understanding?

_____

_____

_____

_____

_____

_____

_____

How have you included Scripture memorizing into your daily routines, and how has it changed your thinking patterns?

_____

_____

_____

_____

_____

_____

_____

_____

Consider the function of creative expression in group study. How has exchanging creative interpretations within a group enhanced the collective knowledge of Scripture?

_____

_____

_____

_____

_____

_____

_____

_____

Consider the balance between own interpretation and external insights, especially from commentary. How have other opinions changed your interpretation?

_____

_____

_____

_____

_____

_____

Give instances of personalized intelligent questions you've created. How have these questions addressed your specific needs and areas of focus?

_____

_____

_____

_____

_____

_____

_____

Beyond the study of Scripture, consider the influence of persistent praying attitudes on your total spiritual path. How has your constant communication with God affected different elements of your life?

_____

_____

_____

_____

_____

_____

_____

What concrete changes have you seen as a result of your purposeful decisions and your developing biblical understanding?

_____

_____

_____

_____

_____

_____

Made in United States
Troutdale, OR
12/31/2024

27467946R00056